SCHOLASTIC

Practice, Practice, Practice!

TIME, MONEY & MEASUREMENT

by Christine Hood

New York • Toronto • London • Auckland • Sydney
Mexico City • New Delhi • Hong Kong • Buenos Aires

Teaching Resources

Scholastic Inc. grants teachers permission to photocopy the reproducible pages in this book for classroom use. No other part of this publication may be reproduced in whole or in part, or stored in a retrieval system, or transmitted in any form or by any means, electronic, mechanical, photocopying, recording, or otherwise, without written permission of the publisher. For information regarding permission, write to Scholastic Professional Books, 557 Broadway, New York, NY 10012.

Cover design by Maria Lilja

Cover and interior illustrations by Teresa Anderko

Interior design by Ellen Matlach for Boultinghouse & Boultinghouse, Inc.

ISBN: 0-439-59729-3

Copyright © 2005 by Christine Hood

All rights reserved. Printed in the U.S.A.

3 4 5 6 7 8 9 10 40 13 12 11 10 09 08 07 06

Contents

Introduction 5
How to Use This Book 6

Time

It Takes Time 7
judging time

Twelve Hours 8
adding hour and half-hour increments

Busy Day 10
using a schedule

Write the Time 11
using time phrases with digital time

Time Match 12
matching clock faces and time phrases

Time for TV 13
using a schedule

Early or Late? 14
comparing times

It's About Time 15
estimating time with analog clocks

Looking Ahead 16
solving word problems with analog clocks

Abby's Animals 17
using a schedule

Passing Time 18
telling elapsed time with analog and digital clocks

Four in a Row 19
solving word problems

Train Trip! 20
using a schedule

Time Change 21
converting time units

Days in a Month 22
identifying the number of days in a month

Calendar Challenge 23
using a calendar

Sensational Seasons 24
relating activities to seasons

Money

Coin Pouch Pairs 25
adding coin values

Pocket Change 26
adding coin values

Who Is It? 27
adding coin values

Money Matchup 28
matching coin values

Piggy Bank Purchases 30
making change

Vegetable Soup 31
computing prices

Pick a Price............ 32
estimating prices

Shark Supper........... 33
adding dollar values

At the Fair............. 34
comparing money values

Exactly Enough......... 35
solving word problems

Cat Cash.............. 36
adding money values

Super Scoops........... 37
computing prices

Earning and Spending....... 38
solving word problems

Pizza Party............ 39
computing prices

Tic-Tac-Cash........... 40
computing money values

Coupon Savings......... 41
solving word problems

More Coupon Savings..... 42
solving word problems

Supermarket Math....... 43
computing prices

Measurement

Rabbit Riddle........... 44
measuring length

Let's Go for a Walk!...... 45
converting nonstandard units to standard units

Easy Estimations........ 46
estimating length

Look All Around........ 47
estimating length

Tiny Train Toys......... 48
measuring in inches and half inches

Foot-Long Addition...... 49
comparing units of length

Metric Measurements..... 50
converting standard units to metric units

Perimeter Puzzler....... 51
finding the perimeter

Saltwater Aquarium...... 52
measuring length and width

Garden Graphs.......... 54
finding the area

A Question of Weight..... 55
choosing appropriate units of weight

The Best Unit........... 56
identifying appropriate units of measure

Let's Compare!.......... 57
comparing units of volume

Temperature Talk........ 58
reading a thermometer

Think About It!......... 59
choosing appropriate units of measure

Estimate It!............ 60
estimating measurements

Measurement Puzzle..... 61
using measurement-related vocabulary

Answer Key............ 62

Introduction

Welcome to *Practice, Practice, Practice! Time, Money & Measurement*. This book is packed with more than 50 reproducible activity sheets that give children practice in the math concepts of time, money, and measurement. The practice pages are flexible and easy to use—kids can complete them at home or in school, independently or in groups. Each activity features appealing illustrations, topics kids enjoy, and simple instructions so that children can work on their own. Pull out these practice pages for quick activities during the school day, or send them home as skill-building homework assignments.

The activities in *Practice, Practice, Practice! Time, Money & Measurement* also coordinate with the standards recommended by the National Council of Teachers of Mathematics (NCTM). Some of the NCTM standards for content and processes covered in this book include numbers and operations; patterns, functions, and algebra; measurement; data analysis, statistics and probability; problem solving; reasoning and proof; communication; connections; and representation.

These pages were designed to appeal to second and third graders. The topics relate to their world and interests: school, sports, pets, favorite foods, family, friends, seasons, shopping, and more! In addition, children will enjoy the variety of formats. They'll play games, shop at a mall, fill an aquarium with animals, crack a secret code, solve a crossword puzzle, and much, much more. Many of the practice pages challenge children to go beyond solving problems that involve time, money, or measurement. For instance, in some of the activities, students will need to use their answers to answer riddles, complete charts, and play games. As further reinforcement, terms such as *more than*, *less than*, *inches*, *feet*, *meters*, *pounds*, *ounces*, and *liter*, as well as different time phrases, are used throughout the book to help children become accustomed to reading and using the math language related to each concept.

For your convenience, activities are organized by difficulty level under each of the three concept areas. Also, a comprehensive answer key is included at the end of the book (pages 62–64). Each practice page is listed by title and page number. This easy reference will allow you or your students to check their completed pages for correct answers.

Whether you use the pages from *Practice, Practice, Practice! Time, Money & Measurement* for homework or class work, they are sure to give your students an enjoyable way to get the extra practice and reinforcement they need to succeed in math!

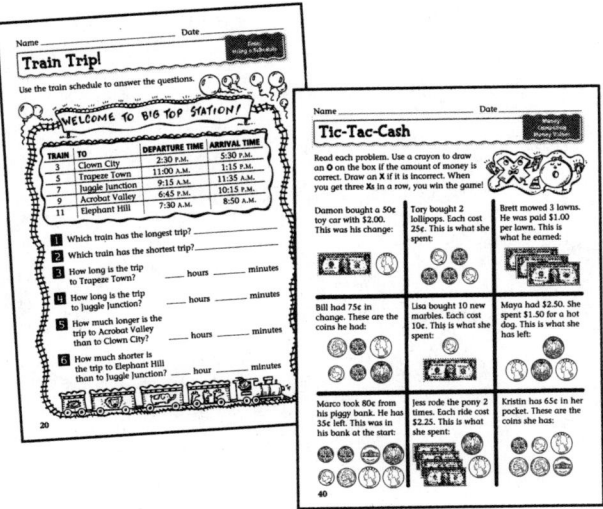

How to Use This Book

These practice pages were designed for flexible use. Children can work on them individually, in pairs, in small groups, or as a whole class. In addition, the ready-to-use pages provide ideal activities to leave for substitute teachers to use with the class. Have students work on the sheets:

- for reinforcement of basic time, money, and measurement concepts
- for review after a math unit is completed
- when they are finished with other class work
- as an activity to start or finish the day
- after lunch to settle back into learning
- as math center activities for practicing skills related to time, money, and measurement concepts
- as skill-building homework activities

Refer to the table of contents to locate the practice pages that address the particular concept that students are working on. For easy reference, the specific skills are also listed in a box near the top of each practice page. You can use the pages in the order they are presented or rearrange them to suit the needs of your students.

Most of the practice pages require only a pencil and eraser. A few require scissors, glue, and crayons. If sending home the sheets as homework, review the directions in advance to answer any questions that children have about the activities. You might also review the materials and modify them if necessary.

When children work on the practice pages independently, encourage them to read the directions and problems carefully before they begin to write on their pages. If desired, you may set up a buddy system, so that children can seek assistance from other classmates if the need arises.

If you plan to use the practice pages in a math center, be sure to place all the materials needed to complete the activities in the center. You may want to make a special folder for the activity pages for each math concept (time, money, and measurement). Include a list of student names and a copy of the answer key for those pages in the folder, too. Then when children visit the center, they can work the assigned practice page, use the answer key to check their work, and check their names off the list to show that they finished the page.

Feel free to modify any of the practice pages to fit your students' specific needs. For example, you might replace some of the half-hour and hour time increments on the Twelve Hours game board and cards (pages 8–9) with different time increments, such as quarter hours. Encourage children to work together and share their problem-solving strategies as they work their way through the practice pages in this book.

Name ______________________ Date ______________________

It Takes Time

Time: Judging Time

Look at the pictures in each box.
Circle the activity that takes the most time.

1

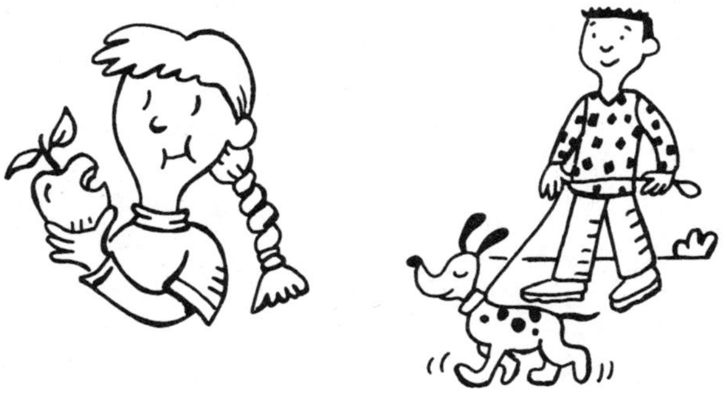

2

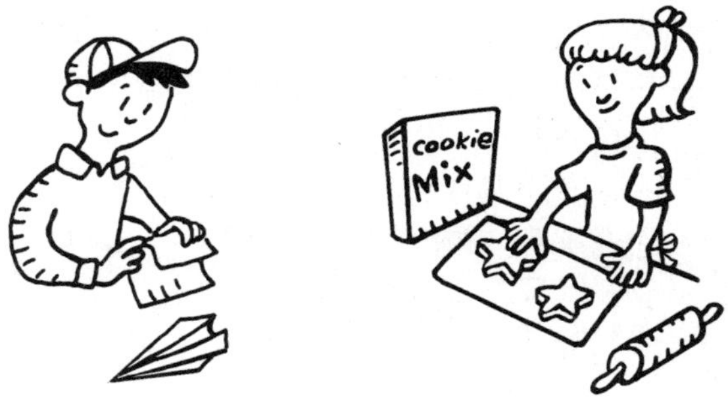

3

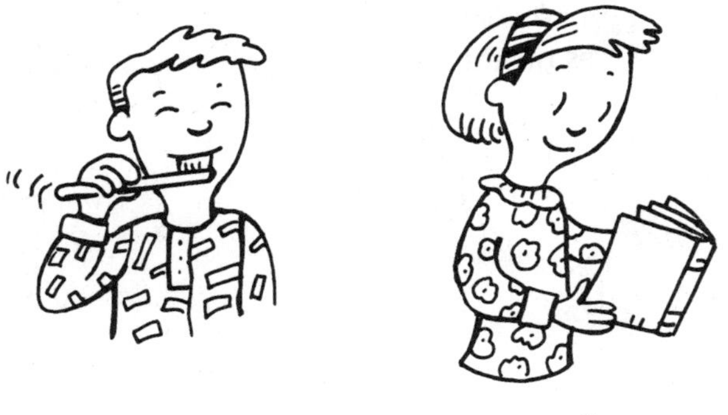

4

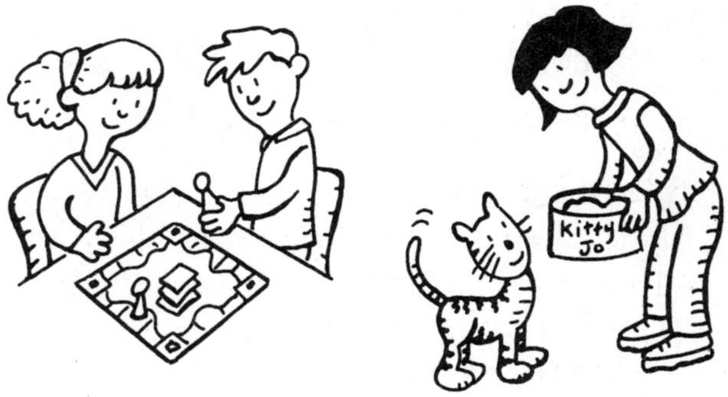

5

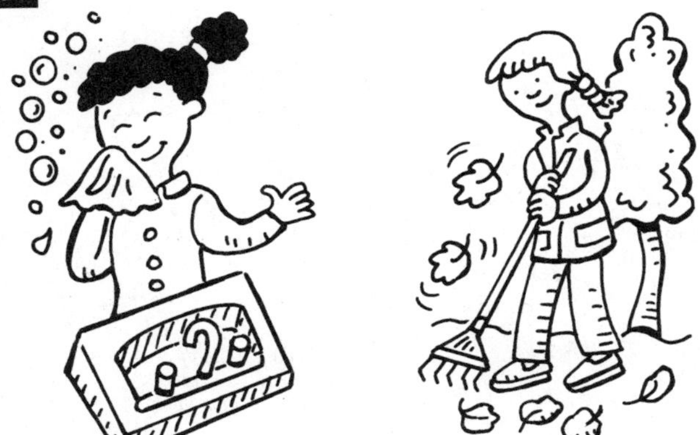

6

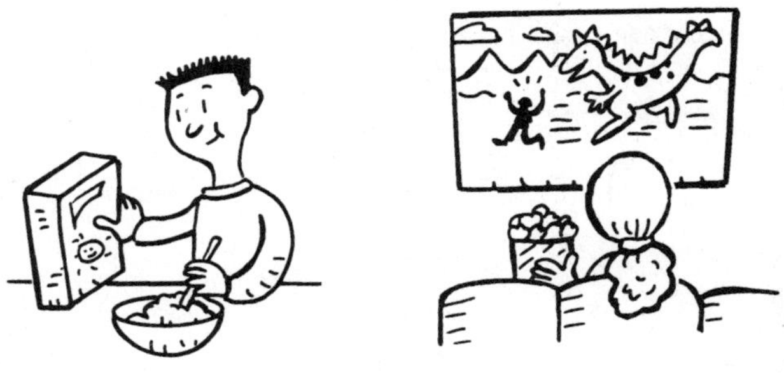

Twelve Hours

Time: Adding Hour and Half-Hour Increments

Invite a friend to play this game with you. First, cut out the game cards on page 9. Shuffle the cards and place them near the game board. Then put a marker for each player on Start (6:00 A.M.).

To play, players take turns picking and reading a card. The player adds that amount of time to the time shown on his or her space. Then the player moves his or her marker to the new time. The first player to reach Finish (6:00 P.M.) wins!

Twelve Hours Game Cards

Walk your dog for 1 hour.	Jump rope for 30 minutes.	Play football for 2 hours.	Run races for 30 minutes.
Talk on the phone for 1 hour.	Paint for 1 hour.	Wash your bike for 30 minutes.	Work a puzzle for 1 hour.
Clean your room for $\frac{1}{2}$ hour.	Play soccer for $1\frac{1}{2}$ hours.	Look for eyeglasses for $\frac{1}{2}$ hour.	Write in your journal for $\frac{1}{2}$ hour.
Help make cookies for 1 hour.	Play with the cat for 1 hour.	Look for crayons for $\frac{1}{2}$ hour.	Play at the beach for 2 hours.
Watch TV for 1 hour.	Play basketball for 30 minutes.	Read for $1\frac{1}{2}$ hours.	Feed the ducks for $\frac{1}{2}$ hour.

Busy Day

Time: Using a Schedule

Mark has a busy day! Use his schedule to answer the questions.

Mark's Schedule

8:30 A.M.	Ride the bus to school
11:45 A.M.	Eat lunch
2:45 P.M.	School ends
3:00 P.M.	Go to after-school art program
4:15 P.M.	Ride the bus home
5:00 P.M.	Walk the dog
5:30 P.M.	Do homework
6:30 P.M.	Eat dinner
7:30 P.M.	Watch TV
8:00 P.M.	Take a bath
9:00 P.M.	Go to bed

1 When does Mark eat lunch? ____:____

2 How much time passes between lunch and the end of school? ____

3 How much time does Mark spend at the after-school art program? ____

4 When does Mark go home? ____:____

5 How long does Mark walk the dog? ____

6 When does Mark watch TV? ____:____

7 How long does he watch TV? ____

Name _____ Date _____

Write the Time

Time: Using Time Phrases With Digital Time

Look at the key to learn some different ways to write the time. Then read the time on each clock. On the lines, write that time in three different ways.

KEY

2:15
15 minutes past 2
a quarter past 2

2:45
15 minutes 'til 3
a quarter 'til 3

1

_____

_____

_____

2

_____

_____

_____

3

_____

_____

_____

4

_____

_____

_____

5

_____

_____

_____

6

_____

_____

_____

11

Name _____ Date _____

Time Match

Time: Matching Clock Faces and Time Phrases

Look at each clock or time phrase on the left.
Find the matching clock or time phrase on the right.
Then draw a line to connect the matching times.

a quarter past 2

11:45

ten o'clock

15 minutes past 6

12

Name _____ Date _____

Time for TV

Time: Using a Schedule

"Gotta See" Weekly TV Schedule

DAY	TIME	SHOW	AIR TIME
Monday	2:30 P.M.	Cartoon Classics	45 minutes
Tuesday	9:30 A.M.	Me and Moe	30 minutes
Wednesday	3:00 P.M.	Video Comics	$1\frac{1}{2}$ hours
Friday	6:15 P.M.	Sports Superstars	45 minutes
Saturday	7:30 A.M.	Leaping Lizards	1 hour
Saturday	11:00 A.M.	School Daze	30 minutes

Use the information from the TV schedule to answer the questions below.

1 Which show airs the longest length of time? _____

2 Which show comes on in the latest part of the day? _____

3 How long will you watch TV if you watch *Cartoon Classics* and *Sports Superstars*? _____

4 How long will you watch TV if you watch *Me and Moe* and *Video Comics*? _____

5 If you watch both shows on Saturday, how long will you watch TV? _____

6 What time does *Sports Superstars* end? _____

7 What time does *Cartoon Classics* end? _____

8 Write three TV shows that have air times that can be added together to equal 2 hours.

_____

_____

Name _____ Date _____

Early or Late?

Time: Comparing Times

Look at the time on each clock. Then read the problem. Circle the correct answer to the question.

1 	The bus picks up children at Sumi's bus stop at 8:15. Is she early or late? early late
2 	Manuel has to meet his brother at the library at 4:00. Is he early or late? early late
3 	Theo's art project is due at 2:15. He just turned it in. Is he early or late? early late
4 	Tana has a 10:30 appointment to walk her friend's dog. Is she early or late? early late
5 	Elena is in a bike race that starts at 9:45. Is she early or late? early late
6 	Ron's speech is scheduled for 11:45. Is he early or late? early late
7 	Brent has a stickball game at noon. Is he early or late? early late
8 	Gia's bedtime is 9:00 P.M. Is she early or late? early late

Name _____   Date _____

It's About Time

Time: Estimating Time With Analog Clocks

Read the time on each clock. Then fill in the circle next to the time that is about the same time shown on the clock.

1. 
- ○ 2:35
- ○ 8:10
- ○ 2:40
- ○ 1:40

2. 
- ○ 12:15
- ○ 11:15
- ○ 3:55
- ○ 11:05

3. 
- ○ 5:30
- ○ 6:25
- ○ 5:35
- ○ 7:30

4. 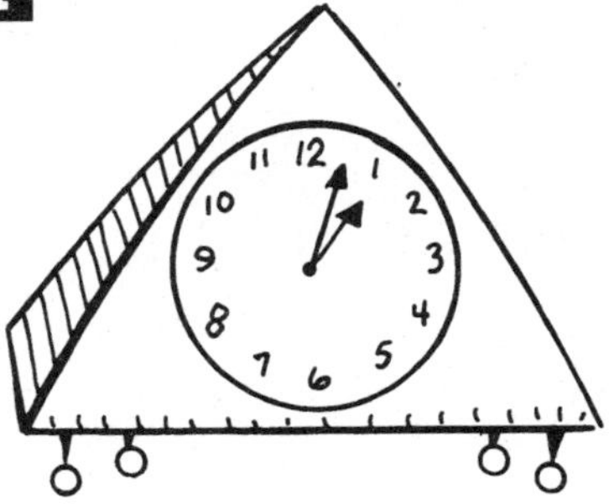
- ○ 1:10
- ○ 2:00
- ○ 12:05
- ○ 1:00

5. 
- ○ 3:20
- ○ 4:15
- ○ 4:20
- ○ 3:30

6. 
- ○ 7:15
- ○ 8:45
- ○ 7:50
- ○ 10:35

7. 
- ○ 8:55
- ○ 9:05
- ○ 11:40
- ○ 11:45

8. 
- ○ 4:00
- ○ 4:04
- ○ 1:20
- ○ 12:20

Name _____ Date _____

Looking Ahead

Time: Solving Word Problems With Analog Clocks

Look at the time on each clock. Then read and solve the problem. Write your answer on the lines. Then draw hands on the blank clock to show that time.

1  It takes Jennie 20 minutes to get to soccer practice.

What time will she get there? _____:_____

2  Parker's mom picks him up after school. School ends in 30 minutes.

What time will she pick him up? _____:_____

3  Kyra talks on the phone for 15 minutes each night.

What time will her phone call end? _____:_____

4  Milo gets washed every Tuesday for 45 minutes.

What time will his bath end? _____:_____

5 Terrance works $1\frac{1}{2}$ hours every Saturday.

What time will he go home? _____:_____

6  Every night, Sasha sings to the moon for 25 minutes.

What time will she stop singing? _____:_____

Name _____ Date _____

Abby's Animals

Time: Using a Schedule

Abby works at the local animal shelter. Use the information from her schedule to answer the questions below.

Daily Schedule for Abby

9:00	Arrive at the shelter
9:15	Feed the birds
9:30	Groom the cats
10:00	Walk the dogs
11:00	Eat lunch
11:30	Clean the rabbit cages
12:10	Feed the dogs and cats
1:30	Go home

1 When does Abby arrive at the shelter? ____:____

2 How long does Abby take to feed the birds? _____

3 Does Abby take more time to groom the cats or to walk the dogs? _____

4 When does Abby eat lunch? ____:____

5 How long does Abby take to clean the rabbit cages? _____

6 When does Abby feed the dogs and cats? ____:____

7 How long does Abby work at the animal shelter each day? _____

Name _____ Date _____

Passing Time

Time: Telling Elapsed Time With Analog and Digital Clocks

Look at the time on both clocks in each box.
Then answer the question.

1   A   B

How much time has passed between Clock A and Clock B?

_____ hour and _____ minutes

2   A   B

How much time has passed between Clock A and Clock B?

_____ hours and _____ minutes

3   A   B

How much time has passed between Clock A and Clock B?

_____ hours and _____ minutes

4   A   B

How much time has passed between Clock A and Clock B?

_____ hours and _____ minutes

5   A   B

How much time has passed between Clock A and Clock B?

_____ hours and _____ minutes

6   A   B

How much time has passed between Clock A and Clock B?

_____ hour and _____ minutes

Four in a Row

Time: Solving Word Problems

Invite a few friends to play this game with you. Ask each player to draw hands on each clock on his or her game board to show a time to the hour or half hour. To play, the caller makes up a simple word problem about time in a country on the game board. For example, the caller might say, "I started climbing a mountain in Mexico at 12:00. I climbed for 2 hours. What time did I stop?"

Each player solves the problem and then checks his or her game card to see if that time is shown under the named country. If so, the player covers that clock with a marker. The first player to cover 4 clocks in a row wins.

19

Name _____ Date _____

Train Trip!

Time: Using a Schedule

Use the train schedule to answer the questions.

WELCOME TO BIG TOP STATION!

TRAIN	TO	DEPARTURE TIME	ARRIVAL TIME
3	Clown City	2:30 P.M.	5:30 P.M.
5	Trapeze Town	11:00 A.M.	1:15 P.M.
7	Juggle Junction	9:15 A.M.	11:35 A.M.
9	Acrobat Valley	6:45 P.M.	10:15 P.M.
11	Elephant Hill	7:30 A.M.	8:50 A.M.

1 Which train has the longest trip? _____

2 Which train has the shortest trip? _____

3 How long is the trip to Trapeze Town? _____ hours _____ minutes

4 How long is the trip to Juggle Junction? _____ hours _____ minutes

5 How much longer is the trip to Acrobat Valley than to Clown City? _____ hours _____ minutes

6 How much shorter is the trip to Elephant Hill than to Juggle Junction? _____ hour _____ minutes

Name _____   Date _____

Time Change

Time: Converting Time Units

Use the information in the key to answer the questions. On the back of the page, show how you got your answers.

KEY
1 minute = 60 seconds   1 year = 365 days
1 hour = 60 minutes   1 year = 52 weeks
1 day = 24 hours   1 year = 12 months
1 week = 7 days

1 Devon practices his guitar 2 hours each day. How many minutes does he practice?

_____ minutes

2 Zora ran the race in 1 minute and 15 seconds. In how many seconds did she finish the race?

_____ seconds

3 McKenzie's little sister is 1 year and 3 months old. How old in months is she?

_____ months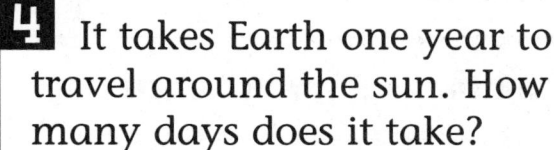

4 It takes Earth one year to travel around the sun. How many days does it take?

_____ days

5 There are 28 days in February this year. How many weeks are in February?

_____ weeks

6 The hike to the top of Pine Mountain takes half a day. How many hours does it take?

_____ hours

7 The movie is 3 hours long. How many minutes long is the movie?

_____ minutes

8 Trey was on a baseball team for 12 weeks. How many days was he on the team?

_____ days

21

Name _____ Date _____

Days in a Month

Time: Identifying the Number of Days in a Month

Read the poem. Then write the correct number of days that are in each month on the chart. Answer the questions at the bottom of the page.

Thirty days hath September,
April, June, and November.
All the rest have thirty-one,
Except for February alone,
Which has twenty-eight each year,
Twenty-nine each leap year.

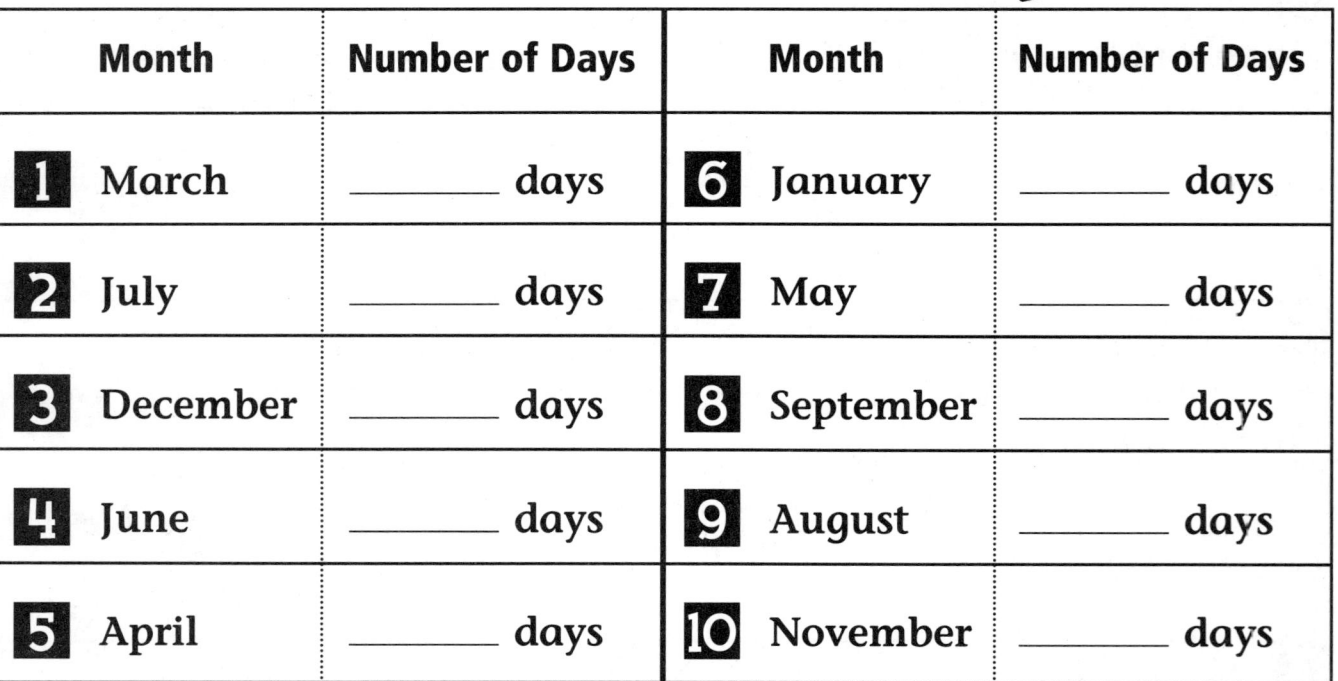

	Month	Number of Days		Month	Number of Days
1	March	_____ days	6	January	_____ days
2	July	_____ days	7	May	_____ days
3	December	_____ days	8	September	_____ days
4	June	_____ days	9	August	_____ days
5	April	_____ days	10	November	_____ days

11 How many days does February have in a leap year? _____ days

12 How many days does February have every other year? _____ days

Name _____ Date _____

Calendar Challenge

Time: Using a Calendar

Use the calendar to answer the questions.

MAY

Sunday	Monday	Tuesday	Wednesday	Thursday	Friday	Saturday
						1
2	3	4	5 Cinco de Mayo	6	7	8
9 Mother's Day	10	11	12	13	14	15
16	17	18	19	20	21	22
23	24	25	26	27	28	29
30	31 Memorial Day					

1 On what day of the week does May begin? _____

2 What is the date of the second Thursday in May? _____

3 On what day of the week is Memorial Day? _____

4 On what day of the week is Cinco de Mayo? _____

5 On what day of the week is the 18th of May? _____

6 What is the date of the fifth Sunday in May? _____

7 On what date is Mother's Day celebrated? _____

8 How many Saturdays are in May? _____

23

Name _____ Date _____

Sensational Seasons

Time: Relating Activities to Seasons

Use the information about the four seasons to answer the questions.

The Four Seasons

- **Winter** — December, January, and February are winter months.
- **Spring** — March, April, and May are spring months.
- **Summer** — June, July, and August are summer months.
- **Fall** — September, October, and November are fall months.

1 The birds chirp while Tessa plants a young tree for Earth Day. As the sun warms her face, Tessa imagines how big her tree will be in ten years. What is the season?

_____

Circle the months in this season:

February
March
April
May
June
July

Draw what you like to do during this season.

2 Josh gets dressed for his snowy walk to school. The Presidents' Day holiday will be celebrated next week. That's the day he will go sledding with his friends! What is the season?

_____

Circle the months in this season:

September
October
November
December
January
February

Draw what you like to do during this season.

3 As Amy rakes the brown leaves in her grandma's yard, she stops to sniff the cool, crisp air. Then she thinks about how she will carve her Halloween pumpkin. What is the season?

_____

Circle the months in this season:

August
September
October
November
December
January

Draw what you like to do during this season.

Name _____ Date _____

Coin Pouch Pairs

Money: Adding Coin Values

Add the value of the coins in each pouch. Write your answers on the lines. Then trace the strings that connect the pairs of pouches, using a different color for each pair. Color the pouch in each pair that has the higher value of coins.

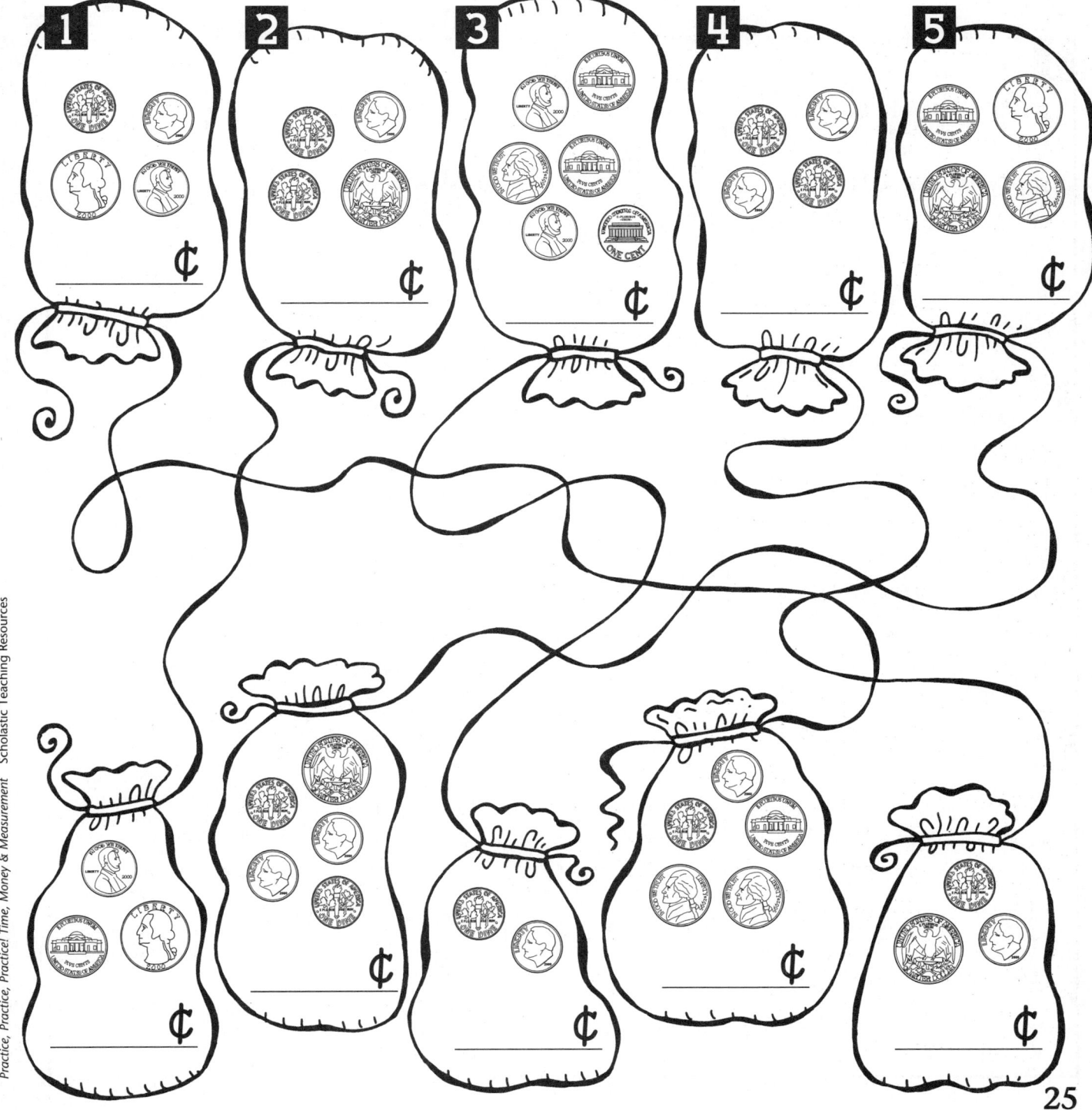

25

Name _____ Date _____

Pocket Change

Money: Adding Coin Values

Use the information in the key to guess which coins are in each pocket. Write the coin names on the lines.

KEY

penny 1¢   nickel 5¢   dime 10¢   quarter 25¢

1 The three coins in this pocket have a value of 25¢. What coins are in the pocket?

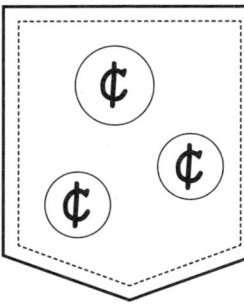

_____
_____
_____
_____

2 The four coins in this pocket have a value of 46¢. What coins are in the pocket?

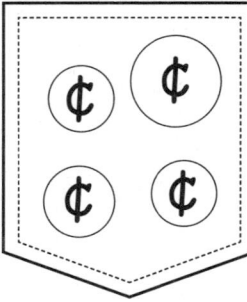

_____
_____
_____
_____

3 The three coins in this pocket have a value of 21¢. What coins are in the pocket?

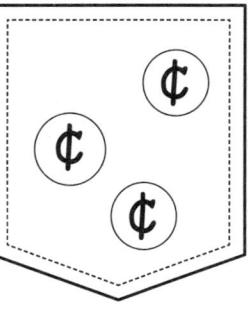

_____
_____
_____
_____

4 The four coins in this pocket have a value of 60¢. What coins are in the pocket?

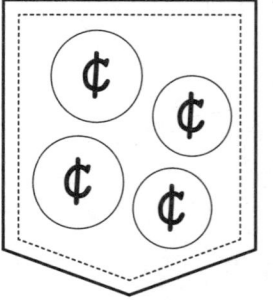

_____
_____
_____
_____

Name _____ Date _____

Who Is It?

Money: Adding Coin Values

Write the value of each set of coins. Then write the number word for that value on the lines. To answer the question, write the circled letters on the lines in the same order as they appear in the problems. Hint: For number words with hyphens, do not write the hyphen(-).

1. _____ ¢
_ _(_)_ _ _ _ _

2. _____ ¢
_(_)_ _ _ _ _

3. _____ ¢
_ _ _(_)_ _ _

4. _____ ¢
_ _ _ _(_)

5. _____ ¢
_(_)_ _ _ _

6. _____ ¢
_ _ _(_)_ _ _ _ _ _ _

7. _____ ¢
_ _ _(_)_ _ _ _ _ _

8. _____ ¢
_ _ _(_)_ _ _ _ _

Question: Whose face is on the one-dollar bill?

Answer: ___ A ___ ___ ___ ___ ___ O ___!

27

Name _____ Date _____

Money Matchup

Money: Matching Coin Values

Invite one or two friends to play this game with you. First cut out all the cards on pages 28 and 29. Then place the cards facedown on a table.

To play, turn over two cards. Add the value of the coins on each card. If the values match, keep the cards. If not, turn them back over. Players take turns until all the matches have been found. The player with the most matches at the end of the game is the winner!

Money Matchup Game Cards

Money Matchup Game Cards

Name _____   Date _____

Piggy Bank Purchases

Money: Making Change

Solve each problem. Write the answer on the piggy bank. Then color the coins needed to equal the value shown on each piggy bank.

1 Drew used the 99¢ in his piggy bank to buy a 25¢ pack of gum. How much change will he put back into his bank?

2 Meg used the 75¢ in her piggy bank to buy a paintbrush for 53¢. How much change will she put back into her bank?

3 Alan used the 82¢ in his piggy bank to buy a 45¢ comic book. How much change will he put back into his bank?

4 Kim used the $1.12 in her piggy bank to buy markers for $1.06. How much change will she put back into her bank?

5 Tyler used the 60¢ in his piggy bank to buy a 39¢ yo-yo. How much change will he put back into his bank?

6 Amber used the 40¢ in her piggy bank to buy a 23¢ postcard stamp. How much change will she put back into her bank?

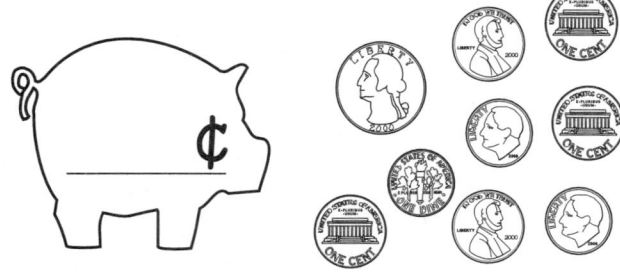

Name _____ Date _____

Vegetable Soup

Money: Computing Prices

Sara needs a lot of vegetables to make soup for her large family! Use the information from the store sign to help Sara find out how much money she needs to buy the vegetables. Then fill in the chart. The first problem has been done for you.

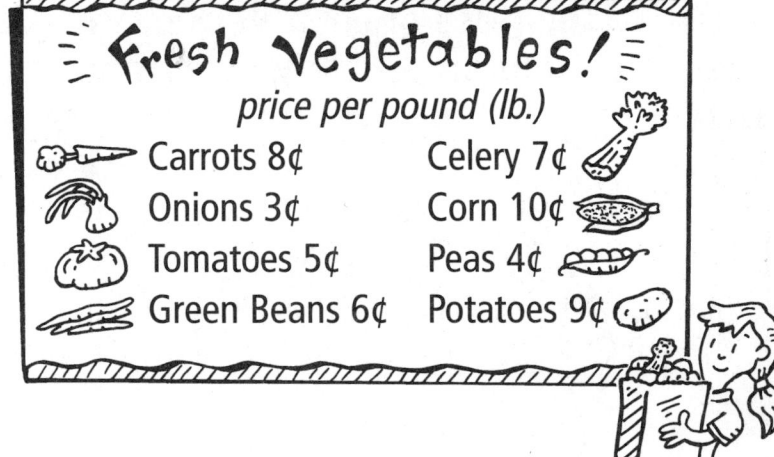

Fresh Vegetables!
price per pound (lb.)
- Carrots 8¢
- Onions 3¢
- Tomatoes 5¢
- Green Beans 6¢
- Celery 7¢
- Corn 10¢
- Peas 4¢
- Potatoes 9¢

What Sara Needs	Write a Problem	What Sara Will Spend
1. 5 lb. of celery	5 lb. × 7¢ = 35¢	35¢
2. 7 lb. of beans		_____
3. 8 lb. of carrots		_____
4. 2 lb. of onions		_____
5. 4 lb. of peas		_____
6. 9 lb. of corn		_____
7. 6 lb. of tomatoes		_____
8. 10 lb. of potatoes		_____

Question: How much will Sara spend all together? _____

Name _____ Date _____

Pick a Price

Money: Estimating Prices

Estimate the price of each item at the All-in-One Department Store. Circle your answer.

1

About how much does a pair of sneakers cost?

$20.00 $2.00   2¢

2

About how much does a candy bar cost?

$40.00 $4.00   40¢

3

About how much does a teddy bear cost?

70¢ $7.00 $70.00

4

About how much does a T-shirt cost?

$10.00   10¢ $100.00

5

About how much does a hamburger meal cost?

$3.00   30¢ $30.00

6

About how much does a book cost?

6¢   60¢ $6.00

Name _____ Date _____

Shark Supper

Money: Adding Dollar Values

The shark family went to the Shining Sea restaurant for a reunion. After supper, the waiter brought each shark a bill. For each problem, look at the bill to see what the shark ordered. Then write the total for the bill.

1 How much is Sarah Shark's supper?

★ SHINING SEA ★
boiled fish eggs $82
seafoam soda   + $6
total $____

2 How much is Sid Shark's supper?

★ SHINING SEA ★
tuna fingers $41
seaweed salad   + $8
total $____

3 How much is Sally Shark's supper?

★ SHINING SEA ★
broiled salmon $52
saltwater tea   + $7
total $____

4 How much is Sam Shark's supper?

★ SHINING SEA ★
squid poppers $64
bubbly water   + $4
total $____

5 How much is Sharif Shark's supper?

★ SHINING SEA ★
shrimp-on-a-stick $72
coral fruit cup   + $6
total $____

6 How much is Shirley Shark's supper?

★ SHINING SEA ★
creamy clam dip $83
algae sticks   + $5
total $____

Name _____   Date _____

At the Fair

Money: Comparing Money Values

The Perez children love going to the fair! Read and solve each problem. Write your answer on the line. Then circle the answer to the question on the right. Use the back of the page to show how you got your answers.

1  Julie has $1.50 in her pocket. How much does she need to buy a hot dog and soda?

_____

Does she have enough money?

Yes   No

2  Rita brought $2.25 to the fair. How much does she need to buy an ice cream cone and two ride tickets?

_____

Does she have enough money?

Yes   No

3  Pedro tucked $1.55 into his sock. How much does he need to buy a stuffed bear and cotton candy?

_____

Does he have enough money?

Yes   No

4  Jane has $1.75 in her purse. How much does she need to buy popcorn and a hat?

_____

Does she have enough money?

Yes   No

5  Ernest brought $2.35 to spend at the fair. How much does he need to buy a T-shirt and jam?

_____

Does he have enough money?

Yes   No

Name _____ Date _____

Exactly Enough

Money: Solving Word Problems

Use the information from the key to solve the problems. Write your answers on the lines.

KEY

penny 1¢   nickel 5¢   dime 10¢   quarter 25¢

1

Betsy has $1.00. What two coins does she need to add to her money to have exactly enough to buy the doll?

_____
_____

2

James has $1.75. What three coins does he need to add to his money to have exactly enough to buy the toy fire truck?

_____
_____

3

Jason needs only 16¢ more to buy a video game. What three coins does he need to have exactly enough money to equal 16¢?

_____
_____
_____

4

Taylor needs only 41¢ more to buy the parrot. What four coins does she need to have exactly enough money to equal 41¢?

_____
_____

35

Name _____ Date _____

Cat Cash

Money: Adding Money Values

Crack the code to learn how much each cat spent. First, use the key to find the money value of each symbol. Write that value in the equation. Add the numbers and then write your answer. Use the back of the page to show how you got your answers.

Cat Cash Key
1¢ = ◆
5¢ = ★
10¢ = ♥
25¢ = ▲
$1.00 = ■

1. Sneaky Cat bought sardines and a toy mouse.
He paid with this cat cash: ■ ▲ ♥ ★

How much did he spend in dollars and cents?

_____ + _____ + _____ + _____ = _____

2. Silky Cat bought a ball of yarn and some fresh cream.
She paid with this cat cash: ■ ▲ ♥ ◆

How much did she spend in dollars and cents?

_____ + _____ + _____ + _____ = _____

3. Snobby Cat bought a new diamond collar.
She spent: ■ ■ ■ ▲ ▲ ★

How much did she spend in dollars and cents?

_____ + _____ + _____ + _____ + _____ + _____ = _____

4. Snippy Cat bought a scratching pole and a water bowl. He spent: ■ ■ ♥ ♥ ◆

How much did he spend in dollars and cents?

_____ + _____ + _____ + _____ + _____ = _____

36

Name _____ Date _____

Super Scoops

Money: Computing Prices

Use the information on the menu to find out how much each ice cream cone costs. Show how you got your answer.

Menu

Ice Cream
- Single scoop 30¢
- Double scoop 60¢
- Triple scoop 85¢

Toppings!
- Candy sprinkles 20¢
- Caramel sauce 35¢
- Cookie rounds 40¢
- Chewy worms 30¢
- Chocolate chips 25¢

1 A double scoop ice cream cone with candy sprinkles and caramel sauce costs _____.

2  A single scoop ice cream cone with chewy worms costs _____.

3  A triple scoop ice cream cone with chocolate chips costs _____.

4  A double scoop ice cream cone with cookie rounds and candy sprinkles costs _____.

5  A triple scoop ice cream cone with caramel sauce, cookie rounds, and chewy worms costs _____.

6  A single scoop ice cream cone with candy sprinkles and chocolate chips costs _____.

37

Name _____ Date _____

Earning and Spending

Money: Solving Word Problems

Solve each word problem. Use the back of the page to show how you got your answers.

1  Mina earned $3.00 raking leaves. Katie earned $2.50 more than Mina. How much money did Katie earn?

$ _____ . _____

2 Chelsea spent 50¢ on a taco. Chris bought 2 more tacos than Chelsea. How much money did Chris spend on tacos?

$ _____ . _____

3  Marty earned $2.00 per hour at the animal shelter. He worked 5 hours this week. How much money did he earn?

$ _____ . _____

4   Kayla earns $4.00 for each horse that she feeds at the stables. She fed 4 horses today. How much did she earn all together?

$ _____ . _____

5   Elisa bought 2 soccer balls for the team. Emilio bought 1 more ball than Elisa. Each ball costs $1.50. How much did Emilio spend on soccer balls?

$ _____ . _____

6  Each ride on the roller coaster costs 25¢. Sue rode 4 times and Cooper rode 8 times. How much did they spend all together on roller coaster rides?

$ _____ . _____

Name _____ Date _____

Pizza Party

Money: Computing Prices

Lana invited seven friends to her pizza party. Each person ordered a pizza with the toppings that he or she liked best. Use the information on the menu to find the price of each pizza. On the back of the page, show how you got your answers.

MENU

Pizza Size

Small	$2.50
Medium	$5.50
Large	$8.00

Toppings (extra)

Pepperoni	$2.00
Onions	$1.00
Mushrooms	$1.25
Extra Cheese	$1.00
Ham	$1.50
Peppers	$1.00
Pineapple	$1.25
Olives	$1.00

1 Lana ordered a small pizza with mushrooms and ham. What is the price of her pizza?

$ _____ . _____

2 Scott ordered a small pizza with onions, extra cheese, and peppers. What is the price of his pizza?

$ _____ . _____

3 Jen and Simon shared a medium pizza with olives and pepperoni. What is the price of their pizza?

$ _____ . _____

4 Tad ordered a medium pizza with extra cheese. What is the price of his pizza?

$ _____ . _____

5 Anna and Darrell shared a large pizza with pineapple. What is the price of their pizza?

$ _____ . _____

6 Tia had a small pizza with ham. After the party, she ordered a large pizza with extra cheese to take to her family. What is the price of her pizzas?

$ _____ . _____

Name _____ Date _____

Tic-Tac-Cash

Money: Computing Money Values

Read each problem. Use a crayon to draw an **O** on the box if the amount of money is correct. Draw an **X** if it is incorrect. When you get three **X**s in a row, you win the game!

Damon bought a 50¢ toy car with $2.00. This was his change:  	Tory bought 2 lollipops. Each cost 25¢. This is what she spent: 	Brett mowed 3 lawns. He was paid $1.00 per lawn. This is what he earned: 
Bill had 75¢ in change. These are the coins he had:      	Lisa bought 10 new marbles. Each cost 10¢. This is what she spent: 	Maya had $2.50. She spent $1.50 for a hot dog. This is what she has left: 
Marco took 80¢ from his piggy bank. He has 35¢ left. This was in his bank at the start:     	Jess rode the pony 2 times. Each ride cost $2.25. This is what she spent: 	Kristin has 65¢ in her pocket. These are the coins she has: 

Name _____ Date _____

Coupon Savings

Money: Solving Word Problems

Use the coupons below to find out how you can save money at the mall. Then answer each question. Use the back of the page to show how you got your answers.

1

How much do two shirts cost?

$ _____ . _____

How much can you save on two shirts with the coupon?

$ _____ . _____

2

How much does one baseball mitt cost?

$ _____ . _____

How much does the mitt cost with the coupon?

$ _____ . _____

3

How much do three books cost?

$ _____ . _____

How much do three books cost with the coupon?

$ _____ . _____

4

How much does a pair of sneakers cost with the coupon?

$ _____ . _____

How much can you save on a pair of sneakers with the coupon?

$ _____ . _____

41

Name _____ Date _____

More Coupon Savings

Money: Solving Word Problems

Use the coupons below to find out how you can save money at the mall. Then answer each question. Use the back of the page to show how you got your answers.

1
How much do a ball and a toy mouse cost?

$ _____ . _____

How much do the ball and toy mouse cost with the coupon?

$ _____ . _____

2

How much do four yo-yos cost?

$ _____ . _____

How much can you save on four yo-yos with the coupon?

$ _____ . _____

3

How much do eight cookies cost?

$ _____ . _____

How much do eight cookies cost with the coupon?

$ _____ . _____

4

How much do two coats cost?

$ _____ . _____

How much can you save on two coats with the coupon?

$ _____ . _____

Name _____ Date _____

Supermarket Math

Money: Computing Prices

Use the information from the sales flyer to answer the questions. On the back of the page, show how you got your answers.

This Week's Specials!

Bananas   30¢ per pound
Apples   60¢ per pound
Peanuts   80¢ per pound
Grapes $1.25 per pound
Fish $1.60 per pound
Steak $2.50 per pound

1 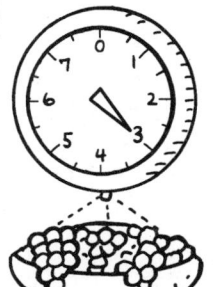 The price of the grapes is _____.

2  The price of the steak is _____.

3  The price of the bananas is _____.

4  The price of the peanuts is _____.

5  The price of the fish is _____.

6  The price of the apples is _____.

43

Name _____ Date _____

Rabbit Riddle

Measurement: Measuring Length

Write the length of each pet. Then look at the key to find the letter for each answer. Unscramble all the letters to solve the rhyming riddle.

KEY
1 = M   4 = U   7 = A   10 = F
2 = B   5 = L   8 = P
3 = R   6 = N   9 = Y

1

Length: ____ units   Letter: ____

2

Length: ____ units   Letter: ____

3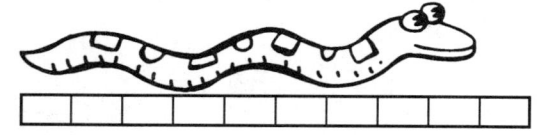

Length: ____ units   Letter: ____

4

Length: ____ units   Letter: ____

5

Length: ____ units   Letter: ____

6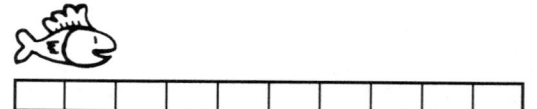

Length: ____ units   Letter: ____

7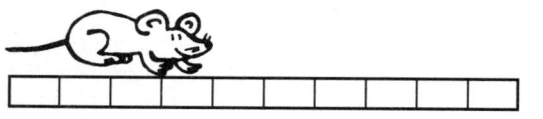

Length: ____ units   Letter: ____

8

Length: ____ units   Letter: ____

Riddle: What do you call a rabbit with a good sense of humor?

Answer: A F ___ ___ ___ N ___ !

Name _____ Date _____

Let's Go for a Walk!

Measurement: Converting Nonstandard Units to Standard Units

It's time to go for a walk, but the Tiny Town dogs have mixed up their leashes. To match the dogs to their leashes, write the length of each leash in units. Then use the information in the key to convert the units to inches. Draw a line from each leash to the dog that wears a leash of the same length.

KEY

4 units = 1 inch

2 units = $\frac{1}{2}$ inch

1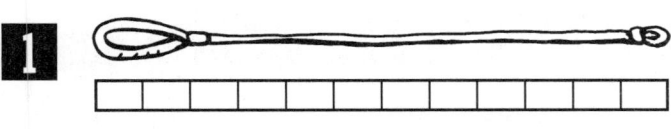

Length: _____ units or _____ inches

A. 1 inch

2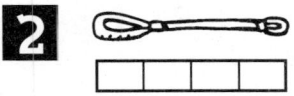

Length: _____ units or _____ inch

B. 4 inches

3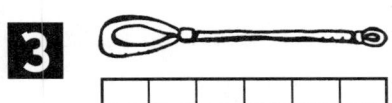

Length: _____ units or _____ inches

C. $2\frac{1}{2}$ inches

4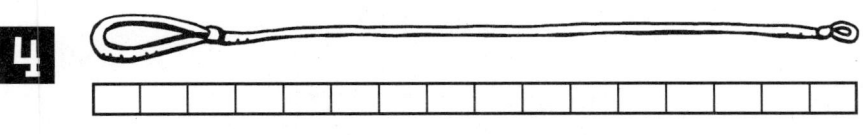

Length: _____ units or _____ inches

D. 3 inches

5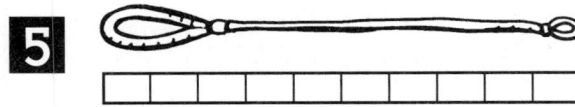

Length: _____ units or _____ inches

E. $1\frac{1}{2}$ inches

Name _____ Date _____

Easy Estimations

Measurement: Estimating Length

Find each object in your classroom. Estimate the length of the object in inches. Then use a ruler to check your estimate. Write your answers. Compare your estimate to the actual length to see if your estimate was correct.

1

Estimate: The glue stick is about _____ inches long.

Measure: The glue stick is actually _____ inches long.

2

Estimate: The marker is about _____ inches long.

Measure: The marker is actually _____ inches long.

3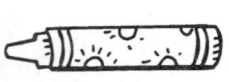

Estimate: My shoe is about _____ inches long.

Measure: My shoe is actually _____ inches long.

4

Estimate: The crayon is about _____ inches long.

Measure: The crayon is actually _____ inches long.

5

Estimate: My hand is about _____ inches long.

Measure: My hand is actually _____ inches long.

6

Estimate: The scissors are about _____ inches long.

Measure: The scissors are actually _____ inches long.

Name _____ Date _____

Look All Around

Measurement: Estimating Length

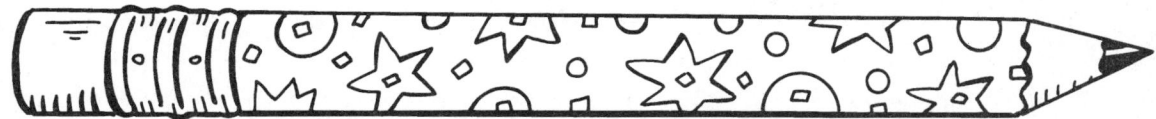

A pencil is about 6 inches long.

Look all around to find three objects that are about 6 inches long. Write the name of each object. Then use a ruler to measure the object. Write the actual length. How close was your estimate?

1 _____ actual length: _____ inches

2 _____ actual length: _____ inches

3 _____ actual length: _____ inches

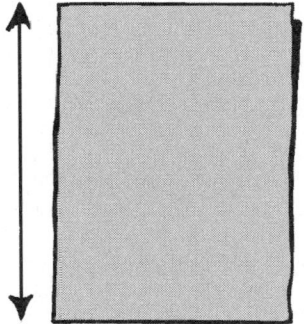

The vertical (tall) side of a sheet of construction paper is about 12 inches (1 foot) long.

Look all around to find three objects that are about 12 inches long. Write the name of each object. Then use a ruler to measure the object. Write the actual length. How close was your estimate?

4 _____ actual length: _____ inches

5 _____ actual length: _____ inches

6 _____ actual length: _____ inches

Name _____ Date _____

Tiny Train Toys

Measurement: Measuring in Inches and Half Inches

Use a ruler to find the longest measurement for each item. Write your answers on the lines.

1

The train is _____ inches long. The train is _____ inch tall.

2

The tree is _____ inch wide.

The tree is _____ inches tall.

3

The station is _____ inches long.

The station is _____ inches tall.

4

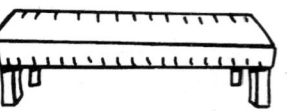

The bench is _____ inches long.

The bench is _____ inch tall.

Name _____ Date _____

Foot-Long Addition

Measurement: Comparing Units of Length

Write the length of each item on the lines. Then solve the equation. Compare each sum to 1 foot. Write < (is less than), > (is greater than), or = (is equal to) in the box to show your answer.

KEY
12 inches (in.) = 1 foot

1.
← 4 in. → ← 3 in. → ← 5 in. →

___ inches + ___ inches + ___ inches = ___ inches

___ inches ☐ 1 foot

2.
← 9 in. → ← 5 in. → ← 2 in. →

___ inches + ___ inches + ___ inches = ___ inches

___ inches ☐ 1 foot

3.
← 8 in. → ← 2 in. → ← 2 in. →

___ inches + ___ inches + ___ inches = ___ inches

___ inches ☐ 1 foot

4.
← 3 in. → ← 5 in. → ← 3 in. →

___ inches + ___ inches + ___ inches = ___ inches

___ inches ☐ 1 foot

Name _____ Date _____

Metric Measurements

Measurement: Converting Standard Units to Metric Units

Some people use the metric measurement system to find the length and height of objects. Use the key to find the measurement in metric units of each item below. Write your answer on the line.

KEY

2.5 centimeters (cm) = about 1 inch

1 meter (m) = about 3 feet

1.5 kilometers (km) = about 1 mile

1

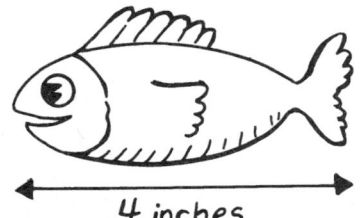

4 inches

The fish is about _____ centimeters long.

2

9 feet

The car is about _____ meters long.

3

6 inches

The mug is about _____ centimeters tall.

4

6 feet

The giraffe's neck is about _____ meters long.

5

3 feet

The boy is about _____ meter tall.

6

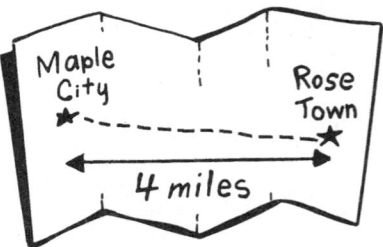

4 miles

The road is about _____ kilometers long.

Name _____ Date _____

Perimeter Puzzler

Measurement: Finding the Perimeter

Find the perimeter of each item. First, write the length of each side to fill in the equation. Then find the sum.

KEY

Perimeter is the distance around an object. It is the sum of the lengths of all its sides.

Example:

The perimeter of this triangle is 6 inches.

2 inches + 2 inches + 2 inches = 6 inches

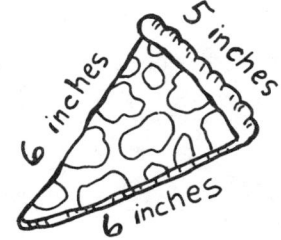

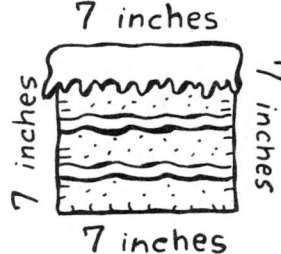

1 The perimeter of the picture frame is ____ inches.

____ inches + ____ inches + ____ inches + ____ inches = ____ inches

2 The perimeter of the book is ____ inches.

____ inches + ____ inches + ____ inches + ____ inches = ____ inches

3 The perimeter of the pizza is ____ inches.

____ inches + ____ inches + ____ inches = ____ inches

4 The perimeter of the cake is ____ inches.

____ inches + ____ inches + ____ inches + ____ inches = ____ inches

Name _____ Date _____

Saltwater Aquarium

Measurement: Measuring Length and Width

These animals live in the aquarium on page 53. To find out where in the aquarium they belong, count the square units in each marked area. Find the animal that fits each space, cut it out, and glue it to the aquarium. On the chart on page 53, find the symbol that matches the symbol next to each animal. Then write how many units long and wide that animal is.

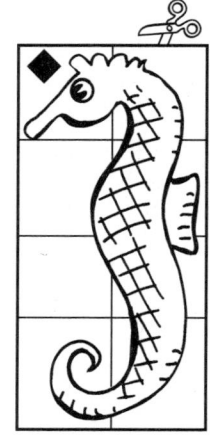

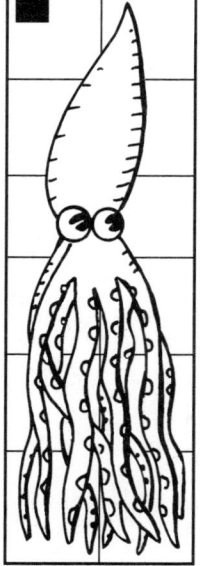

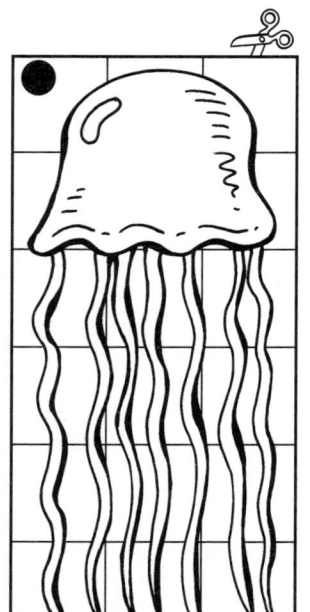

52

Name _____ Date _____

Saltwater Aquarium

Measurement: Measuring Length and Width

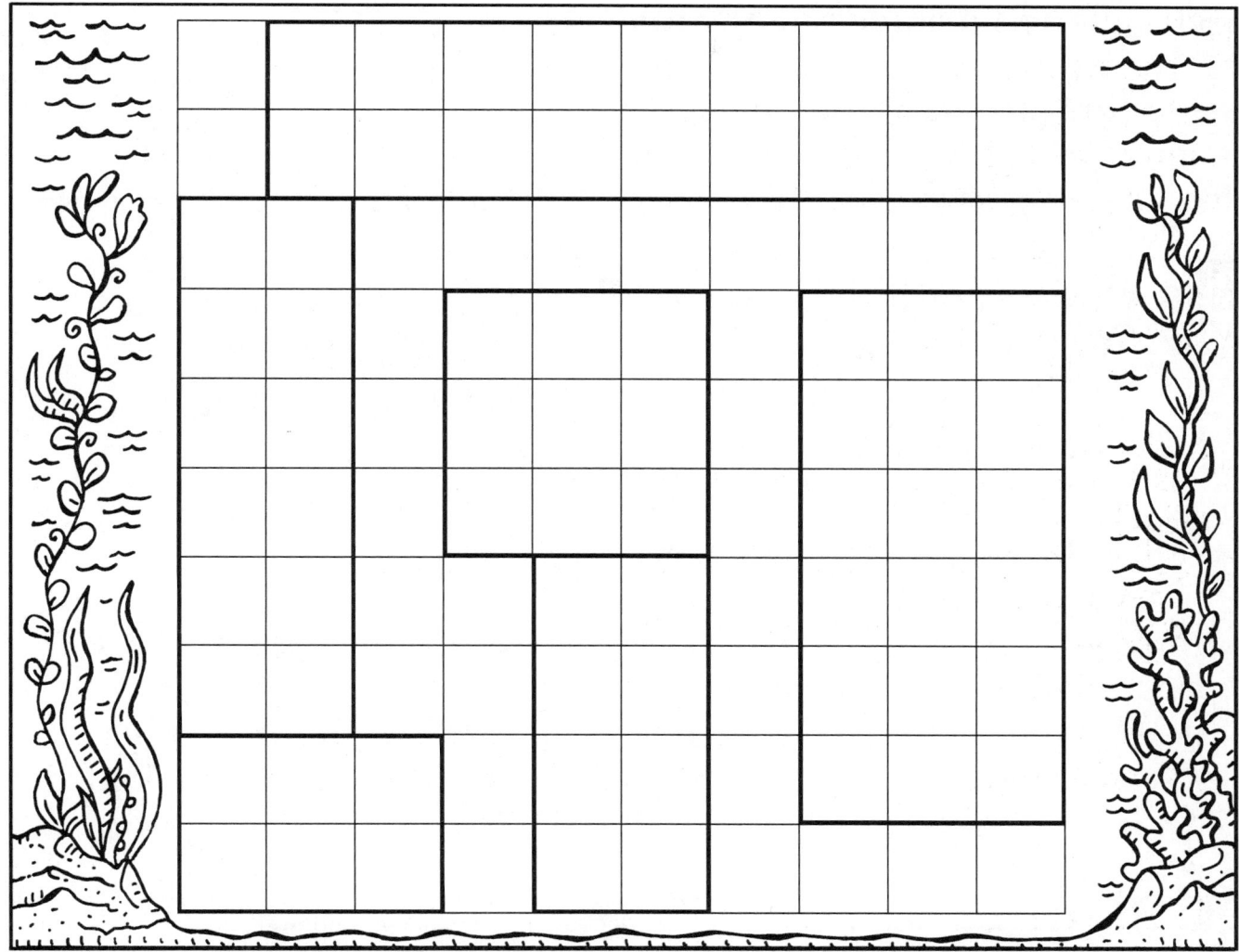

Animal	Units Long	Units Wide
■		
●		
▲		
◆		
♥		
★		

Name _____ Date _____

Garden Graphs

Measurement: Finding the Area

Each child has a garden that is 3 feet by 3 feet. The total area covered by the garden is 9 square feet. Read and solve each problem. Use the key and the garden graph to find your answer.

KEY
☐ = 1 square foot

1
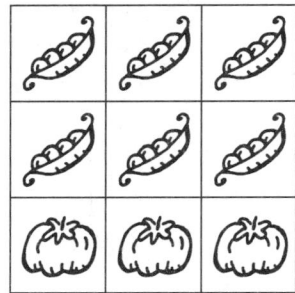

Anthony planted two rows of peas and one row of tomatoes in his garden. What is the area covered by the peas?

_____ square feet

2

Jessica planted 2 square feet of corn and 3 square feet of pumpkins. What area of her garden did she leave unplanted?

_____ square feet

3
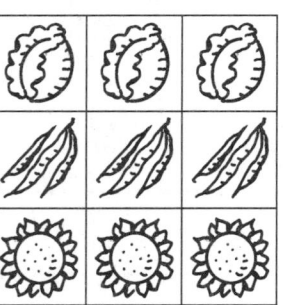

Tim planted one row of lettuce, one row of beans, and one row of sunflowers. What area of his garden is covered by beans?

_____ square feet

4

Viet planted tomatoes in all three rows of her garden. She picked 2 square feet of tomatoes. What area of her garden has tomatoes left?

_____ square feet

54

Name _____ Date _____

A Question of Weight

Measurement: Choosing Appropriate Units of Weight

Ounces are used to measure the weight of very light objects. Pounds are used to measure the weight of heavy objects. Circle the better unit to use to weigh each object below.

KEY

16 ounces = 1 pound

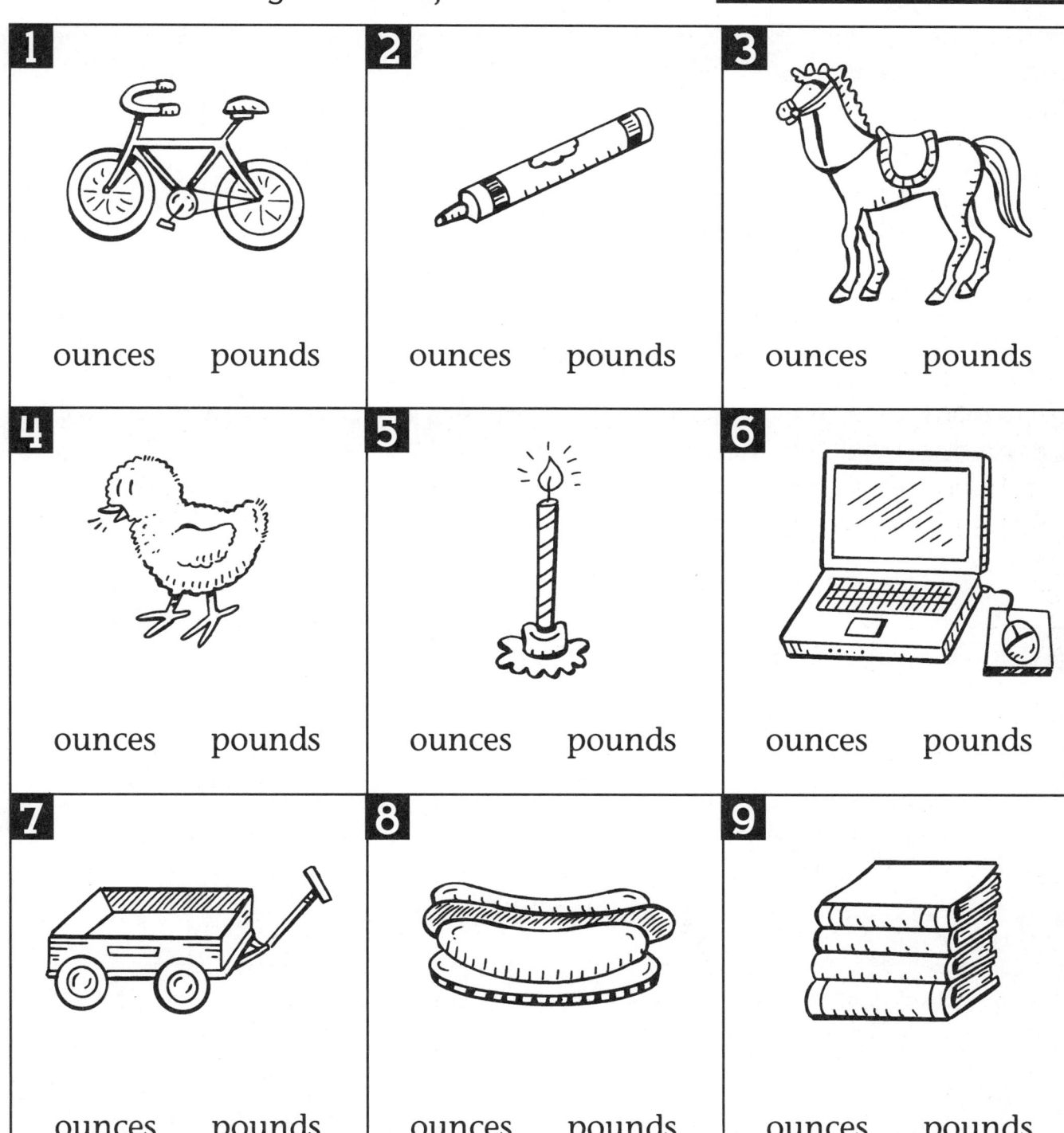

1. bicycle — ounces   pounds
2. crayon — ounces   pounds
3. horse — ounces   pounds
4. chick — ounces   pounds
5. candle — ounces   pounds
6. laptop — ounces   pounds
7. wagon — ounces   pounds
8. hot dog — ounces   pounds
9. books — ounces   pounds

55

Name _____   Date _____

The Best Unit

Measurement: Identifying Appropriate Units of Measure

Cut out the picture cards. Glue each white card under the best unit to use to measure the length of the object. Then glue each gray card under the best unit to use to measure the weight of the object.

LENGTH		
Inches	**Feet**	**Yards**

WEIGHT		
Ounces	**Pounds**	**Tons**

Name _____   Date _____

Let's Compare!

Measurement: Comparing Units of Volume

Use the information in the key to find out how the volumes in each problem compare. Write < (is less than), > (is greater than), or = (is equal to) in the box.

1 2 quarts ☐ 4 pints

2 300 milliliters ☐ 1 quart

3 2 gallons ☐ 2 liters

4 1 pint ☐ 3 cups

5 1 liter ☐ 500 milliliters

6 8 pints ☐ 1 gallon

7 3 cups ☐ 1 liter

8 1 gallon ☐ 3 quarts

VOLUME

Standard Units
2 cups = 1 pint
2 pints = 1 quart
4 quarts = 1 gallon

Metric Units
250 milliliters = about 1 cup
1 liter = about 1 quart

57

Name _____ Date _____

Temperature Talk

Measurement: Reading a Thermometer

Look at the temperature shown on each thermometer.
Then complete the sentences.

1 The temperature is ____°F.

I will wear _____
_____

2 The temperature is ____°F.

I will wear _____
_____

3 The temperature is ____°F.

I will wear _____
_____

4 The temperature is ____°F.

I will wear _____
_____

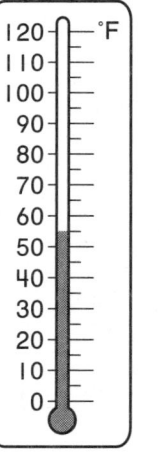

Name _____ Date _____

Think About It!

Measurement: Choosing Appropriate Units of Measure

Read each question. Circle the correct answer.

1 What is the best unit of measure to use to find the height of the lamppost?

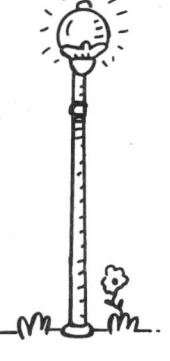

liter   pound   yard

2 What is the best unit of measure to use to find the length of the bread?

mile   foot   meter

3 What is the best unit of measure to use to find how much milk is in the jug?

cup   foot   tablespoon

4 What is the best unit of measure to use to find the temperature?

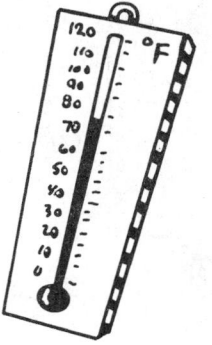

centimeter   pint   degree

5 What is the best unit of measure to use to find the weight of the potatoes?

pound   quart   yard

6 What is the best unit of measure to use to find the distance from Boston to San Francisco?

ton   mile   gallon

Estimate It!

Measurement: Estimating Measurements

Read each question.
Circle the best estimate.

1 About how long is your arm?

    1 foot   1 yard

2 About what is the distance between home and school?

    5 miles   500 miles

3 About how heavy is a cat?

    10 pounds   50 pounds

4 About how long is a crayon?

    15 inches   5 inches

5 About how heavy is a book?

    2 pounds   30 pounds

6 About how wide is your hand?

    7 centimeters   7 meters

7 About how much milk do you drink during a meal?

    1 gallon   1 cup

8 About how wide is your classroom door?

    3 yards   3 feet

9 About what temperature is best for a swim in an outdoor pool?

    90°F   35°F

10 About what temperature is cold enough for a heavy coat?

    28°F   75°F

Measurement Puzzle

Use the key to find the answer to each clue. Write the answer in the puzzle.

KEY
cup
inches
liter
miles
ounces
pounds
quarts
scale
teaspoon
thermometer

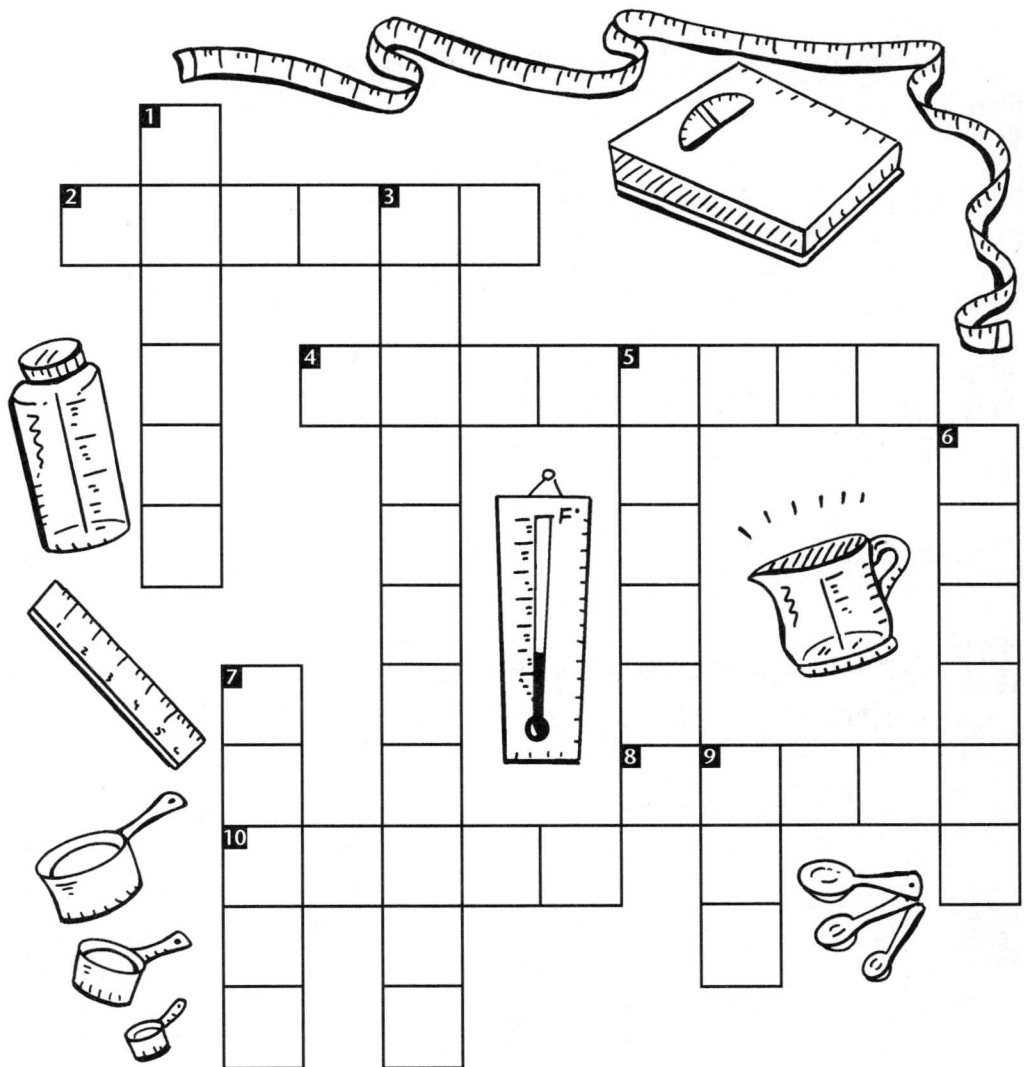

Across

2. Four of these equal 1 gallon
4. Unit used to measure a small amount of salt
8. Tool used to weigh a person
10. Metric unit used to measure volume

Down

1. Units used to weigh a crayon
3. Tool used to take temperature
5. Units used to weigh a dog
6. 12 of these equal 1 foot
7. Units used to measure the distance traveled
9. Unit used to measure milk for recipes

Answer Key

It Takes Time, page 7

The student should circle the following:
1. child walking the dog
2. child making cookies
3. child reading a book
4. children playing a game
5. child raking leaves
6. child at the movies

Twelve Hours, page 8

During play, check to make sure students understand and follow the rules of the game.

Busy Day, page 10
1. 11:45 A.M.
2. 3 hours
3. 1 hour 15 minutes
4. 4:15 P.M.
5. 30 minutes
6. 7:30 P.M.
7. 30 minutes

Write the Time, page 11
1. 7:15, 15 minutes past 7, a quarter past 7
2. 4:45, 15 minutes 'til 5, a quarter 'til 5
3. 10:45, 15 minutes 'til 11, a quarter 'til 11
4. 3:15, 15 minutes past 3, a quarter past 3
5. 1:15, 15 minutes past 1, a quarter past 1
6. 6:45, 15 minutes 'til 7, a quarter 'til 7

Time Match, page 12

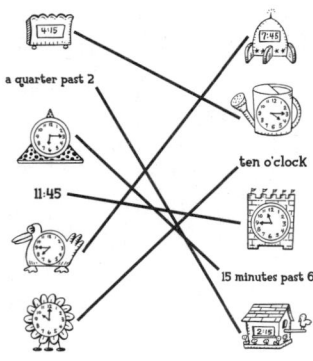

Time for TV, page 13
1. Video Comics
2. Sports Superstars
3. 1 hour 30 minutes (or $1\frac{1}{2}$ hours)
4. 2 hours
5. 1 hour 30 minutes (or $1\frac{1}{2}$ hours)
6. 7:00 P.M.
7. 3:15 P.M.
8. The student should write one of the following combinations of T.V. shows on the lines:
   Cartoon Classics, *Me and Moe*, and *Sports Superstars*
   Cartoon Classics, *Sports Superstars*, and *School Daze*
   Me and Moe, *Leaping Lizards*, and *School Daze*

Early or Late?, page 14

The student should circle the following:
1. late
2. early
3. late
4. early
5. early
6. early
7. late
8. late

It's About Time, page 15
1. 2:40
2. 11:15
3. 5:30
4. 1:00
5. 3:20
6. 7:50
7. 8:55
8. 12:20

Looking Ahead, page 16

1. 8:30

2. 3:15

3. 7:45

4. 5:00

5. 11:30

6. 12:15

Abby's Animals, page 17
1. 9:00
2. 15 minutes
3. walk the dogs
4. 11:00
5. 40 minutes
6. 12:10
7. $4\frac{1}{2}$ hours

Passing Time, page 18
1. 1 hour and 15 minutes
2. 3 hours and 0 minutes
3. 2 hours and 10 minutes
4. 4 hours and 30 minutes
5. 0 hours and 45 minutes
6. 1 hour and 50 minutes

Four in a Row, page 19

During play, check to make sure students understand and follow the rules of the game.

Train Trip!, page 20
1. train 9
2. train 11
3. 2 hours 15 minutes
4. 2 hours 20 minutes
5. 0 hours 30 minutes
6. 1 hour 0 minutes

Time Change, page 21
1. 120 minutes
2. 75 seconds
3. 15 months
4. 365 days
5. 4 weeks
6. 12 hours
7. 180 minutes
8. 84 days

Days in a Month, page 22
1. 31 days
2. 31 days
3. 31 days
4. 30 days
5. 30 days
6. 31 days
7. 31 days
8. 30 days
9. 31 days
10. 30 days
11. 29 days
12. 28 days

Calendar Challenge, page 23
1. Saturday
2. May 13
3. Monday
4. Wednesday
5. Tuesday
6. May 30
7. May 9
8. 5

Sensational Seasons, page 24
1. Spring; The student should circle March, April, and May.
2. Winter; The student should circle December, January, and February.
3. Fall; The student should circle September, October, and November.

Coin Pouch Pairs, page 25
1. Top pouch: 46¢; Bottom pouch: 35¢; The student should color the top pouch.
2. Top pouch: 55¢; Bottom pouch: 31¢; The student should color the top pouch.
3. Top pouch: 18¢; Bottom pouch: 20¢; The student should color the bottom pouch.
4. Top pouch: 40¢; Bottom pouch: 45¢; The student should color the bottom pouch.
5. Top pouch: 60¢; Bottom pouch: 65¢; The student should color the bottom pouch.

Pocket Change, page 26
1. dime, dime, nickel
2. quarter, dime, dime, penny
3. dime, dime, penny
4. quarter, quarter, nickel, nickel

Who Is It? page 27
1. 20¢; twenty
2. 16¢; sixteen
3. 80¢; eighty
4. 50¢; fifty
5. 95¢; ninety-five
6. 18¢; eighteen
7. 32¢; thirty-two
8. 70¢; seventy

Answer: Washington!

Money Matchup, pages 28–29
The matching card pairs have the following coin combinations:

2 quarters; 4 dimes and 2 nickels

2 dimes and 1 nickel; 1 quarter

2 dimes and 2 nickels; 1 quarter and 1 nickel

4 nickels; 1 dime, 1 nickel, and 5 pennies

1 dime and 5 pennies; 3 nickels

3 quarters and 1 dime; 2 quarters, 3 dimes, and 1 nickel

2 dimes, 2 nickels, and 3 pennies; 3 dimes and 3 pennies

2 quarters, 1 dime, and 1 nickel; 1 quarter and 4 dimes

3 quarters; 1 quarter and 5 dimes

Piggy Bank Purchases, page 30
1. 74¢; The student should color 2 quarters, 2 dimes, and 4 pennies.
2. 22¢; The student should color 2 dimes and 2 pennies.
3. 37¢; The student should color 1 quarter, 1 dime, and 2 pennies.
4. 6¢; The student should color 1 nickel and 1 penny.
5. 21¢; The student should color 2 dimes and 1 penny.
6. 17¢; The student should color 1 dime, 1 nickel, and 2 pennies.

Vegetable Soup, page 31
1. 5 lb. × 7¢ = 35¢; 35¢
2. 7 lb. × 6¢ = 42¢; 42¢
3. 8 lb. × 8¢ = 64¢; 64¢
4. 2 lb. × 3¢ = 6¢; 6¢
5. 4 lb. × 4¢ = 16¢; 16¢
6. 9 lb. × 10¢ = 90¢; 90¢
7. 6 lb. × 5¢ = 30¢; 30¢
8. 10 lb. × 9¢ = 90¢; 90¢

Sara will spend $3.73 all together.

Pick a Price, page 32
The student should circle the following:
1. $20.00
2. 40¢
3. $7.00
4. $10.00
5. $3.00
6. $6.00

Note: Other choices may be accepted if the student can explain his or her reasoning.

Shark Supper, page 33
1. $88
2. $49
3. $59
4. $68
5. $78
6. $88

At the Fair, page 34
1. $1.30; yes
2. $1.85; yes
3. $1.61; no
4. $1.84; no
5. $2.32; yes

Exactly Enough, page 35
1. dime, nickel
2. quarter, quarter, quarter
3. dime, nickel, penny
4. quarter, dime, nickel, penny

Cat Cash, page 36
1. $1.00 + 25¢ + 10¢ + 5¢ = $1.40
2. $1.00 + 25¢ + 10¢ + 1¢ = $1.36
3. $1.00 + $1.00 + $1.00 + 25¢ + 25¢ + 5¢ = $3.55
4. $1.00 + $1.00 + 10¢ + 10¢ + 1¢ = $2.21

Super Scoops, page 37
1. $1.15
2. 60¢
3. $1.10
4. $1.20
5. $1.90
6. 75¢

Earning and Spending, page 38
1. $5.50
2. $1.50
3. $10.00
4. $16.00
5. $4.50
6. $3.00

Pizza Party, page 39
1. $5.25
2. $5.50
3. $8.50
4. $6.50
5. $9.25
6. $13.00

Tic-Tac-Cash, page 40

Coupon Savings, page 41
1. $20.00; $10.00
2. $5.25; $4.75
3. $3.00; $2.00
4. $10.00; $2.50

More Coupon Savings, page 42
1. $2.00; $1.50
2. $1.20; $0.40
3. $1.20; $0.90
4. $40.00; $10.00

Supermarket Math, page 43
1. $3.75
2. $5.00
3. $1.20
4. $1.60
5. $4.80
6. $3.00

Rabbit Riddle, page 44
1. 6; N
2. 4; U
3. 9; Y
4. 9; Y
5. 6; N
6. 2; B
7. 4; U
8. 6; N

Riddle Answer: A FUNNY BUNNY!

Let's Go For a Walk, page 45
1. 12 units; 3 inches; The student should draw a line from the leash to dog D.
2. 4 units; 1 inch; The student should draw a line from the leash to dog A.
3. 6 units; $1\frac{1}{2}$ inches; The student should draw a line from the leash to dog E.
4. 16 units; 4 inches; The student should draw a line from the leash to dog B.
5. 10 units; $2\frac{1}{2}$ inches; The student should draw a line from the leash to dog C.

Easy Estimations, page 46
Answers will vary.

Look All Around, page 47
Answers will vary.

Tiny Train Toys, page 48
1. 5 inches long; 1 inch tall
2. 1 inch wide; 3 inches tall
3. 2 inches long; 2 inches tall
4. $1\frac{1}{2}$ inches long; $\frac{1}{2}$ inch tall

Foot-Long Addition, page 49
1. 4 inches + 3 inches + 5 inches = 12 inches; 12 inches = 1 foot
2. 9 inches + 5 inches + 2 inches = 16 inches; 16 inches > 1 foot
3. 8 inches + 2 inches + 2 inches = 12 inches; 12 inches = 1 foot
4. 3 inches + 5 inches + 3 inches = 11 inches; 11 inches < 1 foot

Metric Measurements, page 50
1. 10 centimeters
2. 3 meters
3. 15 centimeters
4. 2 meters
5. 1 meter
6. 6 kilometers

Perimeter Puzzler, page 51
1. 18 inches; 4 inches + 5 inches + 4 inches + 5 inches = 18 inches
2. 26 inches; 5 inches + 8 inches + 5 inches + 8 inches = 26 inches
3. 17 inches; 5 inches + 6 inches + 6 inches = 17 inches
4. 28 inches; 7 inches + 7 inches + 7 inches + 7 inches = 28 inches

Saltwater Aquarium, pages 52–53

Animal	Units Long	Units Wide
■	6	2
●	6	3
▲	3	3
♦	4	2
♥	9	2
★	3	2

Garden Graphs, page 54
1. 6 square feet
2. 4 square feet
3. 3 square feet
4. 7 square feet

A Question of Weight, page 55
1. pounds
2. ounces
3. pounds
4. ounces
5. ounces
6. pounds
7. pounds
8. ounces
9. pounds

The Best Unit, page 56
The student should glue the following white cards on the "Length" chart as shown:

Inches	Feet	Yards
goldfish	window	house
finger	bookshelf	truck
book	person	football field

The student should glue the following gray cards on the "Weight" chart as shown:

Ounces	Pounds	Tons
eraser	cat	whale
cookie	bike	elephant
quarters	bowling ball	airplane

Note: Other choices may be accepted if the student can explain his or her reasoning.

Let's Compare!, page 57
1. =
2. <
3. >
4. <
5. >
6. =
7. <
8. >

Temperature Talk, page 58
1. 25°F; The student should name winter clothing items.
2. 70°F; The student should name spring clothing items.
3. 90°F; The student should name summer clothing items.
4. 55°F; The student should name fall clothing items.

Think About It!, page 59
The student should circle the following:
1. yard
2. foot
3. cup
4. degree
5. pound
6. mile

Estimate It!, page 60
The student should circle the following:
1. 1 foot
2. 5 miles
3. 10 pounds
4. 5 inches
5. 2 pounds
6. 7 centimeters
7. 1 cup
8. 3 feet
9. 90°F
10. 28°F

Measurement Puzzle, page 61
Across:
2. quarts
4. teaspoon
8. scale
10. liter

Down:
1. ounces
3. thermometer
5. pounds
6. inches
7. miles
9. cup

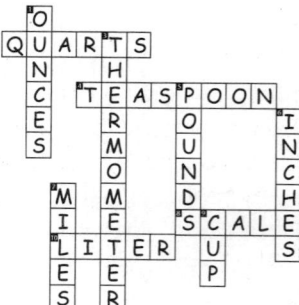